STUDY·GUIDE

Holding on
to your
faith even . . .

WHEN GOD DOESN'T MAKE SENSE

DR. JAMES DOBSON
AMERICA'S FOREMOST FAMILY COUNSELOR

Tyndale House Publishers, Inc.
Wheaton, Illinois

Scripture quotations are taken from the *Holy Bible,* New International Version®.
Copyright © 1973, 1978, 1984 by International Bible Society. Used by permission
of Zondervan Publishing House. All rights reserved. The "NIV" and "New International Version" trademarks are registered in the United States Patent and Trademark Office by International Bible Society. Use of either trademark requires
permission of International Bible Society.

ISBN 0-8423-8239-9

Printed in the United States of America

99 98 97 96 95 94
 7   6   5   4   3   2   1

Contents

How to Use This Study Guide

This subject, perhaps above all others, elicits deep, heartfelt discussion among Christians—and rightfully so! Attempting to understand why things happen the way they do is something that should be pondered. The questions in this brief study guide are designed to help groups and individuals: (1) Discuss the most important stories, quotes, and Scriptures in the book; (2) allow the group to learn from each other's experiences when God didn't seem to make sense.

The leader should give ample time for discussion while moving through each lesson. The sections of this study guide correspond with the chapters in the book and are designed to take between 60 and 90 minutes to complete.

How to Use This Study Guide

WHEN
GOD
DOESN'T
MAKE
SENSE

CHAPTER 1
■
Part A

Key 📖 Story

Chapter 1 opens with a story about a young man with a heart for God and a bright future, who died from leukemia *(see pages 3–5 in the book).*

1. How did this story make you feel?

2. Tell about a situation from your own life, or the lives of others you know, when God didn't seem to make sense.

3. What do you say to people outside the church when they ask you why God allows tragedies to befall those they love or those around the world?

4. What facts do the following Scripture passages point out about God's nature, plan, or character (as listed on pages 8 and 9)?

   • Proverbs 25:2

- Isaiah 45:15

- Deuteronomy 29:29

- Ecclesiastes 11:5

- Isaiah 55:8-9

- Romans 11:33

- 1 Corinthians 2:16

Key  Quote

"Clearly, unless the Lord chooses to explain Himself to us, which often He does not, His motivation and purposes are beyond the reach of mortal man. What this means in practical terms is that many of our questions—especially those that begin with the word *why*—will have to remain unanswered for the time being" *(p. 9)*.

5. Do you think God should be obligated to explain His actions to us?

6. How can a person live with unanswered *whys?*

Key Scripture

"Now we see but a poor reflection as in a mirror; then we shall see face to face. Now I know in part; then I shall know fully, even as I am fully known" *(1 Corinthians 13:12).*

7. Dr. Dobson makes the point that we will not have the total picture until we meet in eternity and that we must learn to accept this partial understanding in faith. If humans were given the chance to know the *whys* of each tragedy they face, what would be the result?

Key Quote

"Unfortunately, many young believers—and some older ones too—do not know that there will be times in every person's life when circumstances don't add up—when God doesn't appear to make sense. This aspect of the Christian faith is not well advertised" *(p. 9).*

8. When you were a new or young Christian, was it well advertised to you that there would be times when circumstances wouldn't add up—that God wouldn't make perfect sense? How was it conveyed?

9. When you hear the phrase "God has a wonderful plan for your life," what does that mean to you?

   □ A life with no pain or heartache
   □ Following Christ no matter what the cost
   □ Holding tightly to the hand of God, taking whatever life dishes out
   □ A middle-class lifestyle
   □ The chance to help others find Him
   □ A fulfilling vocation
   □ Freedom from worry
   □ I don't know
   □ Other:_____

10. What role does your perception of God's character play in whether you blame God or trust Him when tough circumstances arise?

WHEN
GOD
DOESN'T
MAKE
SENSE

CHAPTER 1

■

Part B

Key Quote

"I have found it common for those in crisis to feel great frustration with God. This is particularly true when things happen that seem illogical and inconsistent with what had been taught or understood. Then if the Lord does not rescue them from the circumstances in which they are embroiled, their frustration quickly deteriorates into anger and a sense of abandonment. Finally, disillusionment sets in and the spirit begins to wither" *(p. 12)*.

1. Have you ever felt this kind of frustration? How did you deal with it?

Key Story

The letter from the boy who was burned, then taunted by kids at school, illustrates the common belief that God punishes those He is displeased with by causing a physical ailment to persist in their life *(pp. 12–13)*.

2. Do physical ailments ever mean that a person is being punished by God?

3. Is this belief (that God causes physical ailments to punish people) being used by Satan to turn people away from God?

Key Quote

"Interestingly enough, pain and suffering do not cause the greatest damage [to a person's faith]. *Confusion* is the factor that shreds one's faith" *(p. 13).*

4. Do you find this to be true with those you know?

5. What can be done to help clear up this confusion?

Key Quote

"The human spirit is capable of withstanding enormous discomfort, including the prospect of death, *if the circumstances make sense"* *(p. 13).*

6. The assumption here is that having confidence that God knows what He is doing is much tougher when the circumstances don't make sense. Can we ever get to the point where, even though circumstances don't make sense to us, we can believe with full conviction that they *do* make sense to God?

7. Is this a good goal to pursue?

8. As children grow, their minds ask dozens of questions they cannot possibly understand the answers to. Coming to a conclusion often means *knowing* and *understanding* other foundational facts. If you have children, about what topics have you had to tell them, "You don't understand"?

9. What will it take for them to get to the point where they *will* understand?

   □ Maturity
   □ Time
   □ Teaching
   □ Experience
   □ Other:_____

10. Have you ever felt as if God was saying to you, "But you don't understand"?

Key Scripture

Job makes two statements that serve as a great example to those who choose to trust in God: "Shall we accept good from God, and not trouble?" *(2:10)* **and "Though he slay me, yet will I hope in him"** *(13:15).*

11. How can you get to this level of understanding God's character?

Key Quote

"Apparently, most believers are permitted to go through emotional and spiritual valleys that are designed to test their faith in the crucible of fire" *(p. 17).*

12. Would you agree or disagree with this statement? Why?

13. Describe someone you thought was strong in faith who went through doubt, disillusionment, and despair. How did it happen?

Key Quote

"The Lord can be trusted—even when He can't be tracked" *(p. 21).*

14. If you have children, can they trust you when you can't be tracked (when they don't understand everything you're doing)?

15. Are you able to do the same with God?

THE
BETRAYAL
BARRIER

—

CHAPTER 2
■

1. When facing a moment of crisis, what is normally your attitude?

   □ "Whatever happens, happens."
   □ "I just hope the Lord gives me the grace to handle this."
   □ "I want what would cause the least amount of hassle, grief, and pain."
   □ "I don't mind facing the hard road so I can grow, learn, and help others."
   □ Other:_____

2. When God sent Moses to Pharaoh, Moses questioned God about what His intentions were. (Read Exodus 5:20–6:9.) Was God indifferent, mad, reassuring, or surprised at Moses' question?

3. How do you think God is responding when you question Him?

| Key ✒ Quote |

"Most of us lesser mortals do not do as well [as Moses]. We bail out [of God's plan] before the pieces start fitting together" *(p. 28)*.

4. Why are some Christians so quick to "bail out"?

5. Satan is described as the "father of lies" (John 8:44) and "a roaring lion looking for someone to devour" (1 Peter 5:8). To what extent do you realize this in your life and the lives of those in your family?

Key Story

Dr. Dobson mentions the heartbreaking accounts of the Gustafsons and the parents of Bristol, who lost children at very young ages *(pp. 30–34)*.

6. What is especially difficult about this type of tragedy?

Key Quote

"A loving Father does not tear the heart out of a family for selfish purposes! No, it is better to acknowledge that we have been given too few facts to explain all the heartache in an imperfect, fallen world. That understanding will have to await the coming of the sovereign Lord who promises to set straight all accounts and end all injustice" *(p. 35)*.

7. What are some of the trite phrases people use to explain away tragedy?

Dr. Dobson reminds us of the story of Joseph. "What pleased God was Joseph's faithfulness when nothing made sense" *(p. 36).* **Knowing the end of a story like this brings comfort that God knew exactly what He was doing.**

8. How does knowing the end of Joseph's story bring comfort to you today?

Key ██ Story

Read the story of Yesu on pages 38–39.

9. What possible good could come out of a tragedy like this?

10. Scripture makes it clear that Christians will encounter trouble and trials (see 2 Corinthians 7:4-5 and 1 Peter 4:12-13 on p. 40). Why, then, do some Christians not know of this possibility?

Key Quote

**"My concern is that many believers apparently feel God owes them smooth sailing or at least a full explanation (and perhaps an apology) for the hardships they encounter. We must never forget that He, after all, is *God"* *(pp. 40–41).*

11. What *does* God owe you? (What do you deserve?)

12. What have you been given?

GOD MAKES SENSE EVEN WHEN HE DOESN'T MAKE SENSE

CHAPTER 3
▪
Part A

1. If you remember when you asked the question "Why, God?" for the first time, describe the circumstances.

Dr. Dobson makes a convincing case that emotions can't be trusted. "They lie as often as they tell the truth" *(p. 47)*.

2. If a youth—in the years of emotional instability—makes the emotional decision to make God the bad guy, how will that decision be contradicted or reinforced as he matures into his 20s?

3. Is rejection of faith in God an intellectual or emotional decision?

Key Quote

"**It is typical for vulnerable people to accept what they 'feel' about the Lord at face value. But what they feel may reflect nothing more than a momentary frame of mind. Furthermore, the mind, the body, and the spirit are very close neighbors. One usually catches the ills of the next. If a person is depressed, for example, it affects not only his emotional and physical well-being; his spiritual life suffers too**" *(p. 47).*

4. What can make someone "vulnerable"?

5. If someone rejects their faith when emotionally or physically down, how can they be encouraged to take another, closer look at God?

6. Christians who are raised faithfully in the church occasionally walk away from a faithful God when they feel He doesn't make sense. When is the best time to begin laying an accurate foundation for this issue with children?

7. What should be said?

Key  **Quote**

"Because they [Christians] don't 'feel' His presence, they cannot believe He cares. Since the facts don't add up, they are convinced no reasonable explanation exists. Their prayers bring no immediate relief, so they presume they are not heard. But they are wrong" *(pp. 48–49).*

8. Was there ever a time when you could not *feel* the presence of a parent or friend, then reasoned that that person didn't care?

9. Why do some people do that with God?

10. It has been said that God answers prayer in one of four ways: "yes," "no," "wait," or "I told you that already." Would you agree? Are there other ways God answers prayer?

Dr. Dobson quotes Rev. Reubin Welch, saying, "'With God, even when nothing is happening—*something* is happening'" *(p. 49).*

11. Can you think of an example in your life that illustrates this point?

12. Read:

- Matthew 28:20

- Matthew 18:20

- Proverbs 18:24

- 1 Peter 3:12

- Psalm 139:7-10

Why is it so important to know promises like these?

Key  Quote

"Faith is holding onto uncertainties with passionate conviction'"
(p. 50).

13. Name five aspects of God's character that are the most important for you to cling to:

➤

➤

➤

➤

➤

GOD MAKES SENSE EVEN WHEN HE DOESN'T MAKE SENSE

CHAPTER 3

■

Part B

Key Story

Dr. Dobson tells the story of waiting six years for the dismissal of a lawsuit that was slapped on him after his service on the Attorney General's Commission on Pornography (pp. 53–55). **During those years, he prayed about it, but much of his time was taken up with waiting and preparing for a final decision.**

1. What does it take for someone to become a better "waiter" for God's perfect timing?

2. Do you ever wonder why Jesus didn't help or heal everyone during His stay on earth or why He waited until after age 30 to start His ministry?

3. Name three things that can be learned through waiting and being content.

   ➤

   ➤

   ➤

4. When the good die young and the wicked prosper, what does that tell you of God's economy of priorities?

Key Quote

"For reasons that are impossible to explain, we human beings are incredibly precious to God" *(p. 59).*

5. Why is it hard to realize and feel this all the time?

6. How does God speak words of love to His children?

7. In Luke 11:13, Psalm 103:13, and Isaiah 66:13, God's love for us is illustrated by the parent/child relationship. If you have children, name several parental-type feelings you have toward them:

➤   ➤   ➤

➤   ➤   ➤

➤   ➤   ➤

8. The truth is, God has these same feelings (only magnified) for you. Is it difficult to believe God feels this way about you?

Dr. Dobson tells the story of having to hold down his son, Ryan, so an ear could be treated for infection *(pp. 60–62).*

9. Can you recall a time when your child was hurt and you hurt more seeing his pain—but you knew it was best?

10. Do you think God ever feels this way?

"Your arms are too short to box with God. Don't try it!" *(p. 63).*

11. Why do people try to box with God?

☐ Their God is too small, so they think they have a chance.
☐ Their God is impotent.
☐ Their God isn't actively involved in the affairs of man.
☐ They're mad at themselves for something but can't take responsibility for their actions.
☐ They don't believe God actually exists.
☐ Other:_____

12. How have Christians tried to "take God on" through the centuries?

13. Men and governments have done a number of things to place themselves higher than God (ego, evolution, banning God from public life, etc.). What else has our culture done to "out-think" God?

ACCEPTANCE
OR
DESPAIR

—

CHAPTER 4

■

Key Story

God tested Abraham by waiting to fulfill His promises until the circumstances seemed impossible. Then He tested him again when He told him to sacrifice his only son, Isaac. His faith stayed strong, and he passed both tests.

1. Does God use circumstances to test *your* faith?

2. What is God's reaction if you fail tests He allows into your life?

Key Quote

"Abraham believed God even when God didn't make sense. The facts clearly said, 'It is impossible for this thing to happen.' The Lord had made 'empty promises' for nearly 25 years, and still there was no sign of action. Unanswered questions and troubling contradictions swirled through the air" *(p. 76).*

3. It is human nature to accuse God of not making sense—and getting mad or confused about it—when the circumstances seem "negative" or painful. Why don't people do that when God fails to make sense in ways that *benefit* them?

4. List four of His benefits that don't always make sense.

➤

➤

➤

➤

| Key 📖 Story |

At the top of page 81, as Bob Vernon recounts a story about a rafting trip, he makes the statement, "Don't think about ways to squirm out of trouble. Just stay committed and you'll come through in due course."

5. What type of character qualities does it take to keep this attitude in the forefront of your mind when circumstances are tough? How are those qualities acquired?

Bob Vernon finishes his rafting story by saying that if he had jumped out, he would have been killed. Dr. Dobson then asks the question, "Have you considered jumping into the river and trying to swim to safety on your own? That is precisely what Satan would have you do" *(p. 83)*.

6. Can you think of a time when that has happened in your life?

Read the story by Dr. Conway on pages 83–89.

7. What do you think about Dr. Conway's reaction to his daughter's leg amputation?

In summary to Dr. Conway's situation, Dr. Dobson states, "Don't demand explanations. Don't lean on your ability to understand. Don't turn loose of your faith. But do choose to trust Him, by the exercise of the will He has placed within you. The only other alternative—is despair" *(p. 89)*.

8. Does everyone have the capacity to do this?

"HE WILL DELIVER US, BUT IF NOT..."

CHAPTER 5
■

After talking about a *Newsweek* article that tells what a large percentage of Americans believe in prayer, Dr. Dobson says, "I'm not naive enough to believe that all these praying Americans were seeking a committed relationship with the Living God. For some, prayer is only an inch or two from superstition, such as astrology or any other shot in the dark" *(p. 94).*

1. How do the unchurched view prayer? What does their god look like?

2. Reread the passages listed on page 95. What conclusions about God and prayer can you draw?

3. God is always quick to hear but sometimes slow to answer. Are there situations in your home where you are quick to hear the request of your child but slow to answer? (For example, Christmas and birthday present requests, daily "I wants," or rewards for a job well done.)

4. God invites us to prayer. How would you feel as a parent if you encouraged your child to talk with you often—yet he or she never took the time to do so? Does God feel this way about our refusal to accept His invitation?

5. Would you ever give up making that offer to your children? Would God?

6. Dr. Dobson tells the story of when his family prayed for provision during a particularly lean time (pp. 97–98). Recall times in your own life or family when God did miraculous things.

| Key Story |

The principal character in the book *Of Human Bondage* was a young man with a clubfoot. Discovering Christianity, he prayed and hoped God would take away his infirmity. When He didn't, "he felt his faith had been invalidated, and he lost interest in God" *(p. 100)*.

7. Have you ever known anyone who didn't stick with God because He didn't play Santa Claus?

Key Quote

"Consider for a moment the kind of world it would be if God did exactly what we demanded in every instance. . . . The entire basis for the God-man relationship would be undermined. People would seek a friendship with Him in order to gain the fringe benefits, rather than responding with a heart of repentance and love. Indeed, the most greedy among us would be the first to be drawn to the benefits of the Christian life. Most importantly, these evidences of God's awesome power would eliminate the need for faith" *(pp. 101–2).*

8. It is obvious that God is selective in how He answers prayer based on what is needed for long-term growth and character development. How can you have a heart and attitude that will let Him do that for you without becoming resentful?

9. Moses thought he had an insurmountable weakness in his slowness of tongue, yet God chose to use him anyway. How can weakness be used by God as a strength if you are a servant of God?

10. Are you more attracted to people who seem perfect (have many "strengths") or by those more on your own level (who have weaknesses)? Why?

"Most will admit to having an 'if only' that keeps life from being ideal" *(p. 105)*.

11. What are some of the "if onlys" in your life?

12. Many use those two words often, especially during the middle or later seasons of their lives. Why are those two words so destructive?

"'Heaven is not *here*, it's *There*. If we were given all we wanted here, our hearts would settle for this world rather than the next. God is forever luring us up and away from this one, wooing us to Himself and His still invisible Kingdom where we will certainly find what we so keenly long for'" *(p. 106)*.

13. Is the realization that this earth is not heaven an effective way to help cope with negative circumstances?

This chapter points to the passage in Daniel 3:17-18: "The God we serve is able to save us from it, and he will rescue us from your hand, O king. But even if he does not, we want you to know, O king, that we will not serve your gods or worship the image of gold you have set up."

14. In all honesty, have you come to this conclusion in your own life?

QUESTIONS
AND
ANSWERS

———

CHAPTER 6

■

Key Quote

"He [God] will always be the determiner of what is best for those who serve Him" *(p. 117)*. **This statement was in response to the woman whose son was healed of a heart problem, but whose husband died of cancer.**

1. How do you feel about God being the determiner of what is best for you?

2. God is sovereign. Discuss what that means to you.

Key Quote

"I'm convinced that faith in moments of crisis is insufficient, unless we are also willing to trust our very lives to His care. That is a learned response, and some people find it more difficult than others by reason of temperament" *(p. 121)*.

3. Would you agree that temperament plays a role in our ability to trust God?

Key Quote

"Our faith must be grounded in a solid commitment of the will, in our prayer life, and in a careful study of Scripture" *(p. 122)*.

4. Talk about how each of these should "flesh out" in your own life for you to have the type of trust necessary to withstand major and minor trials.

5. Jesus' ministry was characterized by periods of exhilaration and ordeals that would be terrible to encounter (a 40-day battle with Satan, for instance). It seems that these types of ups and downs were planned for Him ahead of time. What circumstances cause your life to go "up" and "down"?

Key Quote

"There is often a quiet awareness in the midst of chaos that the Lord is there and He is still in control" *(p. 125)*.

6. Share a time when you felt this "quiet awareness" of God's presence.

Key Story

Dr. Dobson tells the story of his heart attack in August of 1990. Though he initially didn't take the pain in his chest too seriously, he soon realized the seriousness of the situation. He says, "I had lived my life in such a way as to be ready for that moment [when he might die]" *(p. 129)*.

7. What is included in being ready for the moment of your death?

8. Read Romans 8:28-39 and Psalm 73:23-26. Why are passages like this so significant for the Christian going through tough circumstances?

9. Romans 8:28 has often been used as the "super-verse" to help explain tough times that Christians face. Dr. Dobson says this passage must be interpreted from an eternal perspective, rather than a temporal, earthbound point of view. What does this mean?

10. What happens when Christians get angry or disillusioned with God for everything bad that happens instead of trying to look at things through His eyes? What do they potentially miss out on?

THE
ADVERSITY
PRINCIPLE

—

CHAPTER 7
■

Key Quote

Dr. Dobson quotes Albert Einstein after Einstein's students guessed they knew 2 percent of the knowledge in the universe. "'I think your guesses are high, but I'll accept that figure of 2 percent. Now tell me, what are the chances that God exists in the other 98?'" *(p. 144).*

1. Of the people you know who are choosing not to follow Christ, what are their main reasons, and how do you respond?

Key Story

Astrophysicist Dr. Stephen Hawking began to enjoy life after he was diagnosed with ALS syndrome. He said, "When one's expectations are reduced to zero, one really appreciates everything that one does have" *(p. 146).*

2. What would have to happen in your life to help you realize that each small pleasure is precious?

Key Quote

"An individual in crisis will either grow stronger or become demoralized. Within certain limits, of course, adversity can have a positive effect on people by helping to build character" *(p. 147).*

3. Can you think of someone you know whom this relates to?

4. Why is perseverance such an important quality to acquire? (Read James 1:2-4; Romans 5:3-4; 2 Timothy 4:6-8; and Revelation 2:7, 11, 17, 26-28; 3:5, 12, 21.)

Key  Quote

"Consider a tree planted in a rain forest. Because water is readily available, it does not have to extend its root system more than a few feet below the surface. Consequently, it is often poorly anchored and can be toppled by a minor windstorm. But a mesquite tree planted in a hostile and arid land must send its roots down 30 feet or more in search of water. . . . Its unfriendly habitat actually contributes to stability and vigor" *(p. 147).*

5. Did anyone ever teach you this "adversity principle"? If so, what did you think when they did?

"If it is accurate to say that hard times often lead to emotional and physical toughness, then the opposite must also be valid. And, indeed, it is. Easy living and abundance often produce a certain underlying weakness" *(p. 150).*

6. If the culture is soft, does that mean the church within it is soft, as well?

7. Can the church grow stronger without opposition? Can you?

8. Confidence in our ability to trust God is gained through small steps of experience. What smaller trials did Jesus' disciples go through that gave them the courage to trust God amid the larger trials they would experience after Jesus returned to the Father? (See pp. 156–58.)

9. Can you think of some other trials the disciples went through, besides the ones Dr. Dobson mentions?

Key Quote

"For seven hours, Jesus watched the disciples do battle with a severe head wind before He came to assist them. Yet they were in His vision and under His care throughout the night. Obviously, He permitted them to experience their need before coming to their rescue" *(p. 157)*.

10. Why was it a good idea for Jesus to wait?

Key Quote

"Flabby, overindulged, pampered Christians just don't have the stamina to fight this battle" *(p. 161)*.

11. How can we overcome a lack of stamina to fight the spiritual battles God would have us enter into?

FAITH
MUST BE
TOUGH

—

CHAPTER 8

■

Key Story

The Civil War letter from Major Sullivan Ballou to his wife a week before he was killed at the first battle of Bull Run *(pp. 168–69)* was particularly moving. It illustrates the willing sacrifices people have gone through for the sake of earthly kingdoms. "Is this the level of dedication and sacrifice to which the apostle Paul calls us in 2 Timothy 2?" Dr. Dobson asks. "I believe it is, yet the concept seems almost unreasonable in this day of individual rights and self-fulfillment" *(p. 170)*.

1. Share an experience from your life (or the life of someone you know) when you felt this kind of dedication.

Key Scripture

"Endure hardship with us like a good soldier of Christ Jesus. No one serving as a soldier gets involved in civilian affairs—he wants to please his commanding officer" *(2 Timothy 2:3-4)*.

2. What "hardships" do most Western Christians face? How do they "endure" them?

Key Quote

Reread the words of the song "Jesus, I My Cross Have Taken" from page 171. This message is different from many of the songs sung in the church today, "and it may even be unpalatable to a modern world. But it is biblically accurate, and you can build a rock-solid foundation of faith on it. With it, you can cope with whatever life throws at you, even when God makes absolutely no sense" *(p. 172)*.

3. Is this type of message so foreign to people today that they will not swallow it?

4. Are people looking for a cause to die for, a philosophy that fits a selfish lifestyle, or something in between? Why?

5. When tough circumstances have come into your life, have you ever been able to say, "What does it matter? God is God, and there is no doubting His love for me"? If so, did it give you the "peace that transcends understanding" or a gnawing doubt about God's true motives and concern?

Key Quote

"Will we permit the Lord to use our weakness, our disability, our disappointment, our inadequacy, to accomplish His purposes?" *(p. 175)*.

6. This question needs to be answered by every Christian. Can you recall anyone from the Bible who answered yes to these questions? What were the results of making that choice of the will?

Key Scripture

"Rejoice in the Lord always. I will say it again: Rejoice! Let your gentleness be evident to all. The Lord is near. Do not be anxious about anything, but in everything, by prayer and petition, with thanksgiving, present your requests to God. And the peace of God, which transcends all understanding, will guard your hearts and your minds in Christ Jesus" *(Philippians 4:4-7)*.

7. Write down three principles for thriving when God doesn't make sense.

   ➤

   ➤

   ➤

8. Why is keeping our eyes fixed on Jesus (Hebrews 12:1-3) and setting our minds on things above (Colossians 3:1-4) the best strategy for a Christian?

THE
WAGES
OF
SIN

CHAPTER 9

∎

Key Scripture

"Each one is tempted when, by his own evil desire, he is dragged away and enticed. Then, after desire has conceived, it gives birth to sin; and sin, when it is full-grown, gives birth to death" *(James 1:14-15).*

1. Embracing sin is like a cancer. Why are those who are outside of fellowship with God so quick to blame Him for their problems, especially since *they have chosen* to embrace sin?

2. Man's sin and greed has led to wars, millions of aborted babies, and sexually transmitted diseases. Many years ago *Time* magazine pointed out that a "new morality" was sweeping the church. How has this "new morality" affected your life or the lives of those in your family?

3. Can anything be done to recapture biblical morality in this culture?

4. The statistics on sexually transmitted diseases are shocking. Who will have to bear much of the consequences for this "sexual liberation" disaster?

Key Scripture

"The Lord brought me [wisdom] forth as the first of his works, before his deeds of old; I was appointed from eternity, from the beginning, before the world began. When there were no oceans, I was given birth, when there were no springs abounding with water; before the mountains were settled in place, before the hills, I was given birth, before he made the earth or its fields or any of the dust of the world. I was there when he set the heavens in place, when he marked out the horizon on the face of the deep, when he established the clouds above and fixed securely the fountains of the deep, when he gave the sea its boundary so the waters would not overstep his command, and when he marked out the foundations of the earth. Then I was the craftsman at his side. I was filled with delight day after day, rejoicing always in his presence, rejoicing in his whole world and delighting in mankind. Now then, my sons, listen to me; blessed are those who keep my ways. Listen to my instruction and be wise; do not ignore it. Blessed is the man who listens to me, watching daily at my doors, waiting at my doorway. For whoever finds me finds life and receives favor from the LORD. But whoever fails to find me harms himself; all who hate me love death" *(Proverbs 8:22-36).*

5. What strikes you most about wisdom's role in creation?

6. What are the rewards and consequences laid out in the last few verses?

REWARDS | CONSEQUENCES

Key Quote

"I believe many of the trials and tribulations that come our way are of our own making. Some are the direct consequence of sin, as we have seen. In other cases, the pain we experience is a result of unwise decisions. We make such a mess of our lives by foolishness and irresponsibility" *(p. 192).*

7. What trials have you had to face due to your own sin?

8. What trials have you endured due to the sin of family members?

9. What trials have you gone through due to the sin of strangers?

10. Because God doesn't rescue everyone from every trial, some people have concluded He doesn't care—or even exist. Why do you think God has chosen to allow this misperception on the part of the very ones He created and died for? Did He have any other options?

11. Why do people obey physical laws (like not jumping off a 10-story building) but ignore moral ones?

Key Quote

"Satan has unleashed all his fury. He is fostering hate and deceit and aggression wherever human interests collide. He especially despises the institution of the family, which is symbolic of the relationship between Jesus Christ and His church" *(p. 195)*.

12. List five ways Satan is attacking the family.

➤

➤

➤

➤

➤

MORE
QUESTIONS
AND
ANSWERS

CHAPTER 10
■

Key Quote

"I only know that God honors the prayers of His righteous followers, and we should stay on our faces before Him until each child has been granted every opportunity to repent. We must remember, however, that God will not ride roughshod over the will of any individual. He deals respectfully with each person and seeks to attract him or her to Himself. It is wrong, therefore, to blame God if that process takes years to accomplish—or even if it never comes to pass. That is the price of freedom" *(p. 203).*

1. It's often easy to put God on a deadline when it comes to answering prayer. What types of requests do people tend to want God to answer right away?

2. In reality God's willingness to give mankind the choice to accept or reject Him is one of the clearest evidences of His love. Why is this hard to understand?

3. Self-sufficiency is an attitude with destructive consequences. Just like the rich farmer in Luke 12:18-20, Christians are tempted to think life will roll along unencumbered by tragedy. How do you deal with that temptation?

| Key | Scripture |

In Daniel 10:10-13, Daniel is given a vision of the unseen world and the conflict between good and evil that occurs there: "A hand touched me and set me trembling on my hands and knees. He said, 'Daniel, you who are highly esteemed, consider carefully the words I am about to speak to you. . . . Since the first day that you set your mind to gain understanding and to humble yourself before your God, your words were heard, and I have come in response to them. But the prince of the Persian kingdom resisted me twenty-one days. Then Michael, one of the chief princes, came to help me, because I was detained there with the king of Persia."

4. How can you become more aware of the spiritual realm and how it influences your thoughts about God's true nature?

5. The passages listed below refer to this spiritual realm, as well.

- Ephesians 6:12

- 1 John 4:4

- 2 Kings 6:15-17

- Psalm 34:7

- Psalm 91:11

Why is it that prayer doesn't really seem like battle?

Key Story

Dr. Dobson recounts the probabilities of an accident he witnessed on a southern California freeway. Reread that story from pages 216–17.

6. When do you most realize that your life hangs by a thread?

Key Quote

"The bottom line is that our welfare on this mortal coil is influenced by forces that are beyond the scope of our intellect. We are caught up in a struggle between good and evil that plays a significant, although unidentified, role in our lives. Our task, then, is not to decipher exactly how these pieces fit and what it all means, but to remain faithful and obedient to Him who knows all mysteries" *(p. 218).*

7. Given the realities of the spiritual world, how should you act or think in order to not lose sight of this picture?

BEYOND THE BETRAYAL BARRIER

CHAPTER 11

.

1. Since faith is believing that which has no absolute proof (Hebrews 11:1), what are ways you can exercise and strengthen the faith that is so essential to pleasing God?

Key Scripture

"Some faced jeers and flogging, while still others were chained and put in prison. They were stoned; they were sawed in two; they were put to death by the sword. They went about in sheepskins and goatskins, destitute, persecuted and mistreated—the world was not worthy of them. They wandered in deserts and mountains, and in caves and holes in the ground. These were all commended for their faith, yet none of them received what had been promised. God had planned something better for us so that only together with us would they be made perfect" *(Hebrews 11:36-40).*

2. What would you conclude about your life if these circumstances described above happened to you?

   ☐ God is mad at me.
   ☐ God doesn't exist.
   ☐ God counts me worthy to suffer these things.
   ☐ My prayer life isn't good enough.
   ☐ There must be sin in my life.
   ☐ God will use these things for His glory.
   ☐ Other:_____

Key Story

The story of the three cancer patients as told on page 224 illustrates an important point: People usually die as they lived. The words the pastor said on his final Sunday in church were so true *(p. 225).*

3. Why is it that some Christians can respond with such hope and confidence, yet others shake their fist at God?

Key Scripture

Death is often the one tragedy we just can't comprehend. Isaiah 57:1 states, "The righteous perish, and no one ponders it in his heart; devout men are taken away, and no one understands that the righteous are taken away to be spared from evil." And Psalm 116:15 says, "Precious in the sight of the Lord is the death of his saints."

4. Do these passages change your view of death?

5. Seeing Jesus Christ face-to-face is a triumph, not a tragedy. Even knowing this, we'd all like to experience this triumph as late in life as possible. How can we develop a "just passing through" mentality so that trials and circumstances don't cause us to discard our faith?

Key Quote

"No, I can't provide tidy little solutions to all of life's annoying inconsistencies. That will not occur until we see the Lord face-to-face" *(p. 235).*

6. What inconsistencies are still hard for you to live with?

7. Is there anything still preventing you from trusting that God knows the end of the story and will be with you even when you can't feel Him—even when you don't think He makes sense?

Key Scripture

At some point in his life, David was able to say, "For as high as the heavens are above the earth, so great is his love for those who fear him" *(Psalm 103:11)*. **We know the struggles he faced; we know the questions he asked the Lord. Yet we also can read this type of rock-solid truth.**

8. Can you struggle with God and question your circumstances without losing your love and appreciation for Him? How?

9. Do you agree that God is not the source of your pain, that He is the best friend mankind has ever had? If not, what prevents you from believing this?

10. If you are blaming God for some of the ways your life has progressed, can you set aside your bitterness about those heartaches that are charged to His account? Do you need to be reconciled to God and realize afresh the freedom that comes when the past is laid to rest?

Additional titles from Dr. James Dobson

WHEN GOD DOESN'T MAKES SENSE 0-8423-8227-5
An assurance of God's constant care when circumstances
are beyond our control.
Available on Tyndale Living Audio 0-8423-7430-2

THE NEW DARE TO DISCIPLINE 0-8423-0507-6
Best-selling advice on helping children become mature,
responsible adults.
Available on Tyndale Living Audio 0-8423-7429-9

DISCIPLINE WITH LOVE 0-8423-0665-X
Excerpts from the classic *Dare to Discipline*.

DR. DOBSON ANSWERS YOUR QUESTIONS 0-8423-0580-7
Responses to common questions about home and family.

**DR. DOBSON ANSWERS YOUR QUESTIONS:
CONFIDENT FAMILIES** 0-8423-1105-X
Practical advice on anger, depression, self-esteem, and more.

**DR. DOBSON ANSWERS YOUR QUESTIONS:
MARRIAGE & SEXUALITY** 0-8423-1106-8
Practical advice on romance, conflict, gender differences, and more.

**DR. DOBSON ANSWERS YOUR QUESTIONS:
RAISING CHILDREN** 0-8423-1104-1
Practical advice on spirituality, adolescence, discipline, and more.

THE STRONG-WILLED CHILD 0-8423-5924-9
Learn to discipline a child without breaking his spirit.

**WHAT WIVES WISH THEIR HUSBANDS KNEW
ABOUT WOMEN** 0-8423-7896-0
Wise, humorous insights for both spouses on marital happiness.